I0017931

Arduino Starter Book

Unleashing The Power Of Electronic Modules & Sensors

FIRST EDITION

Charles Obinju

Table Content

- LEDs: Light Emitting Diodes for visual feedback.
- Push Buttons: Input buttons for user interaction.
- Potentiometers: Adjustable resistors for analog input.
- Servo Motors: Small motors for precise control.
- Stepper Motors: Motors that move in discrete steps.
- DC Motors: Simple motors for basic motion.
- Ultrasonic Sensors: Measures distance using sound waves.
- IR Sensors: Infrared sensors for detecting objects.
- Temperature Sensors: Measures temperature.
- Humidity Sensors: Measures humidity in the air.
- Light Sensors: Measures ambient light intensity.
- Sound Sensors: Detects sound levels.
- Gas Sensors: Detects various gases in the environment.
- Accelerometers: Measures acceleration.
- Gyroscope Sensors: Measures orientation and rotation.
- Compass Modules: Measures direction using magnetism.
- RFID Modules: Reads RFID tags for identification.
- Bluetooth Modules: Adds Bluetooth communication.
- Wi-Fi Modules: Adds Wi-Fi communication.
- GSM/GPRS Modules: Enables cellular communication.
- GPS Modules: Receives GPS signals for location tracking.
- LCD Displays: Displays information using text and graphics.
- OLED Displays: Organic LED displays with high contrast.

INTRODUCTION

In the realm of electronics and microcontrollers, the Arduino platform stands as a beacon of innovation, enabling countless makers, tinkerers, and inventors to bring their ideas to life. It serves as the canvas upon which limitless possibilities can be painted, turning mere imagination into tangible reality. But what gives Arduino its remarkable versatility? What are the secret ingredients behind its power? The answer, dear reader, lies in the vast array of electronic modules that can be seamlessly integrated into your Arduino projects.

Imagine being able to measure environmental parameters with precision, capture and process data, control motors and actuators with finesse, and communicate wirelessly across distances. The key to unlocking all of these capabilities and more is an in-depth understanding of the electronic modules that can be paired with your Arduino board.

In "Arduino Starter Book: Unleashing the Power of Electronic Modules & Sensors," we embark on a journey through a world of sensors, actuators, and communication devices. Each chapter delves into a specific module, explaining its functionality, usage, and integration with Arduino. We provide hands-on examples and practical projects that not only demonstrate the module's potential but also inspire you to create your own innovations.

From LEDs that light up your imagination to GPS modules that guide your adventures, from servo motors that bring motion to life to Wi-Fi and Bluetooth modules that connect your projects to the digital world, this book covers a wide spectrum of electronic components.

Whether you're a beginner looking to explore the world of Arduino or an experienced maker seeking to expand your toolkit, "Arduino Starter Book" equips you with the knowledge and confidence to tackle projects of increasing complexity. With each module you master, you take a step closer to realizing your most ambitious ideas.

Join us as we embark on this exciting journey through the electronic modules and Sensors used with Arduino. Together, we'll unlock the boundless potential of this remarkable platform and breathe life into your creative visions.

Are you ready to dive in? Let's begin.

This introduction sets the stage for an educational and inspiring book that explores the diverse world of electronic modules used with Arduino, providing readers with the knowledge and tools to excel in their Arduino projects.

ARDUINO UNO PIN OUT CONNECTION

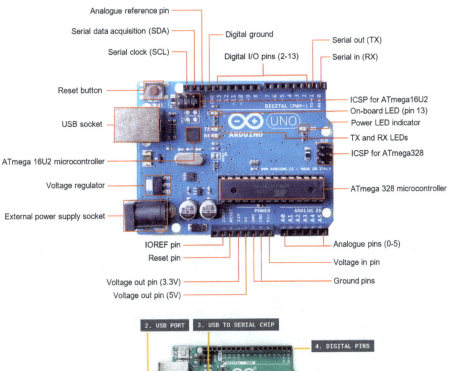

- Analogue reference pin
- Serial data acquisition (SDA)
- Serial clock (SCL)
- Digital ground
- Digital I/O pins (2-13)
- Serial out (TX)
- Serial in (RX)
- Reset button
- USB socket
- ATmega 16U2 microcontroller
- Voltage regulator
- External power supply socket
- ICSP for ATmega16U2
- On-board LED (pin 13)
- Power LED indicator
- TX and RX LEDs
- ICSP for ATmega328
- ATmega 328 microcontroller
- IOREF pin
- Reset pin
- Voltage out pin (3.3V)
- Voltage out pin (5V)
- Analogue pins (0-5)
- Voltage in pin
- Ground pins

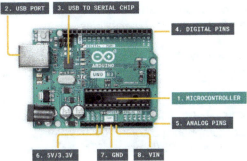

- 2. USB PORT
- 3. USB TO SERIAL CHIP
- 4. DIGITAL PINS
- 1. MICROCONTROLLER
- 5. ANALOG PINS
- 6. 5V/3.3V
- 7. GND
- 8. VIN

ARDUINO FAMILY

ARDUINO NANO   ARDUINO MEGA   ARDUINO LEONARDO

ARDUINO UNO   ARDUINO YUN

ARDUINO FAMILY

The Arduino family consists of a variety of microcontroller boards and related products designed for different applications and user preferences. As of my last knowledge update in September 2021, here are some popular members of the Arduino family:

- **Arduino Uno:** The Arduino Uno is one of the most popular Arduino boards. It features the ATmega328P microcontroller and is a great choice for beginners due to its simplicity and large community support.

- **Arduino Nano:** The Arduino Nano is a compact and versatile board. It's similar to the Uno but in a smaller form factor, making it suitable for projects with limited space.

- **Arduino Mega:** The Arduino Mega is a larger board with more I/O pins and memory. It's often used for more complex projects that require a greater number of inputs and outputs.

- **Arduino Due:** The Arduino Due is based on the powerful ARM Cortex-M3 SAM3X8E microcontroller. It provides more processing power and is suitable for advanced projects and applications.

- **Arduino Leonardo:** The Arduino Leonardo uses the ATmega32U4 microcontroller and is known for its native USB support. It's often used for projects that require USB HID (Human Interface Device) capabilities.

- **Arduino Pro Mini:** The Arduino Pro Mini is a compact, minimalistic board designed for embedded applications. It lacks a built-in USB interface, making it more suitable for permanent installations.

- **Arduino MKR Series:** The MKR series includes various Arduino boards that feature low-power consumption and connectivity options such as Wi-Fi, Bluetooth, and LoRa. They are ideal for IoT (Internet of Things) projects.

- **Arduino Esplora:** The Arduino Esplora is a unique board with built-in sensors and a gamepad-like interface. It's designed for gaming and interactive projects.

- **Arduino IoT Cloud:** This is a cloud-based platform provided by Arduino for building Internet of Things projects. It offers easy connectivity and remote control of your Arduino devices.

- **Arduino Shields:** Arduino Shields are add-on boards that can be stacked on top of Arduino boards to add extra functionality. There are shields available for various purposes, such as Ethernet connectivity, motor control, and more.

- **Arduino Starter Kits:** Arduino Starter Kits are packages that include an Arduino board along with various sensors, components, and a guidebook to help beginners get started with electronics and programming

Common Modules & Sensors

Setting Up Arduino

Setting up an Arduino is a straightforward process. Arduino is an open-source electronics platform that allows you to create interactive projects. Here's a step-by-step guide to help you set up your Arduino:

Step 1: Gather Your Materials

Before you begin, make sure you have the necessary materials:

- Arduino board (e.g., Arduino Uno, Arduino Nano, Arduino Mega, etc.)
- USB cable (usually USB-A to USB-B)
- A computer (Windows, Mac, or Linux)

Step 2: Download the Arduino IDE

The Arduino IDE (Integrated Development Environment) is the software used to write, compile, and upload code to your Arduino board. Follow these steps to download and install it:

- Visit the official Arduino website at **https://www.arduino.cc/en/software.**
- Download the appropriate version of the Arduino IDE for your operating system (Windows, macOS, or Linux).
- Install the Arduino IDE by following the installation instructions provided on the website.

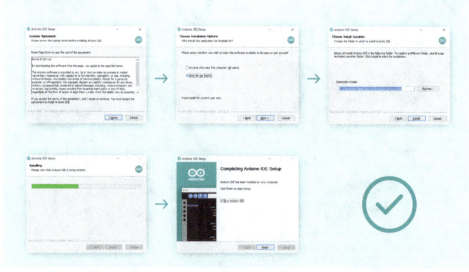

Step 3: Connect Your Arduino Board

Now that you have the Arduino IDE installed, it's time to connect your Arduino board to your computer:

- Plug one end of the USB cable into your Arduino board's USB port.
- Plug the other end of the USB cable into a USB port on your computer.

Step 4: Install Arduino Drivers (Windows Only)

If you're using Windows, you may need to install drivers for your Arduino board. Windows should automatically detect and install the drivers, but if not, follow these steps:

- Open the Arduino IDE.
- Go to "Tools" > "Port" and select the COM port corresponding to your Arduino (it should appear as something like "COM3" or "COM4").

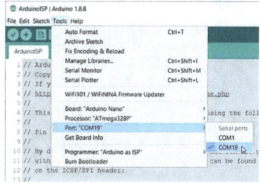

Step 5: Select Your Arduino Board

Before you can start programming your Arduino, you need to select the correct board model:
- In the Arduino IDE, go to "Tools" > "Board" and select your specific Arduino model (e.g., Arduino Uno, Arduino Nano, etc.).

Step 6: Select Your Arduino's COM Port

Choose the COM port that corresponds to your connected Arduino:
- In the Arduino IDE, go to "Tools" > "Port" and select the COM port that your Arduino is connected to (the one you identified in Step 4, if using Windows).

Step 7: Upload Your First Sketch (Program)

Now you're ready to upload your first program (known as a sketch) to your Arduino:
- Open the Arduino IDE.
- Go to "File" > "Examples" > "01.Basics" > "Blink" to open a simple example program that makes an LED on your Arduino board blink.
- Click the "Upload" button (right arrow icon) to compile and upload the program to your Arduino board. You should see "Done uploading" when it's finished.

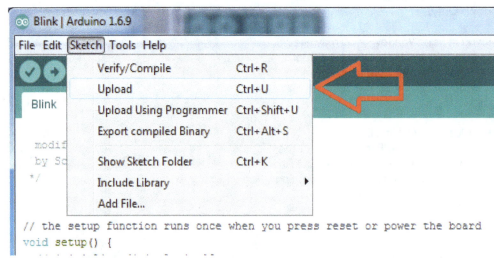

Step 8: Verify Your Arduino is Working

If everything went smoothly, you should see the onboard LED on your Arduino (usually labeled "L" or "13") blinking. Congratulations! You've successfully set up your Arduino.
- You can now start exploring the world of Arduino by creating your own projects and writing custom code. Continue learning and experimenting to unlock the full potential of your Arduino board.

LEDs: Light Emitting Diodes for visual feedback.

LEDs (Light Emitting Diodes) are among the most common electronic components used for visual feedback in Arduino projects. They are easy to work with and can provide various forms of visual indications. Here's a bit more detail on using LEDs with Arduino:

1. **Single LED:** You can simply connect an LED to an Arduino pin through a current-limiting resistor to prevent excessive current flow. This way, you can control the LED's on and off states using Arduino code.
2. **Blinking LED:** This is often the first project for beginners. You can use the delay() function to create a blinking effect with an LED.

Illustration 1

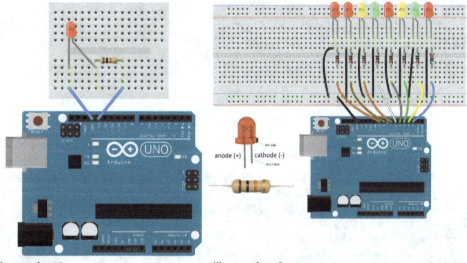

Illustration 1   Illustration 2

{code example 1}

```
1.    const int ledPin = 13; // Pin where the LED is connected
2.
3.    void setup() {
4.      pinMode(ledPin, OUTPUT); // Set the LED pin as an output
5.    }
6.
7.    void loop() {
8.      digitalWrite(ledPin, HIGH); // Turn on the LED
9.      delay(1000); // Wait for 1 second
10.     digitalWrite(ledPin, LOW); // Turn off the LED
11.     delay(1000); // Wait for 1 second
12.   }
```

1. **Multiple LEDs:** You can control multiple LEDs individually by connecting them to different pins and using similar code.

Illustration 2

{code example 2}

```
1.   const int ledPin1 = 13; // Pin for the first LED
2.   const int ledPin2 = 12; // Pin for the second LED
3.
4.   void setup() {
5.    pinMode(ledPin1, OUTPUT);
6.    pinMode(ledPin2, OUTPUT);
7.   }
8.
9.   void loop() {
10.   digitalWrite(ledPin1, HIGH); // Turn on the first LED
11.   delay(500); // Wait for 0.5 second
12.   digitalWrite(ledPin1, LOW); // Turn off the first LED
13.
14.   digitalWrite(ledPin2, HIGH); // Turn on the second LED
15.   delay(500); // Wait for 0.5 second
16.   digitalWrite(ledPin2, LOW); // Turn off the second LED
17.  }
```

1. **PWM Control:** Arduino pins labeled with a tilde (~) support Pulse Width Modulation (PWM). This allows you to create analog-like brightness control for LEDs.

{code example 3}

```
1.   const int ledPin = 9; // Pin where the LED is connected
2.
3.   void setup() {
4.    pinMode(ledPin, OUTPUT);
5.   }
6.
7.   void loop() {
8.    for (int brightness = 0; brightness <= 255; brightness++) {
9.     analogWrite(ledPin, brightness); // Set LED brightness
10.    delay(10); // Small delay for smooth transition
11.   }
12.
13.   for (int brightness = 255; brightness >= 0; brightness--) {
14.    analogWrite(ledPin, brightness);
15.    delay(10);
16.   }
17.  }
```

1. **RGB LEDs:** These have red, green, and blue components in a single package, allowing you to create a wide range of colors.
2. **Addressable LEDs (WS2812B, APA102):** These LEDs can be individually controlled and can create complex patterns and effects. Libraries like FastLED or Adafruit NeoPixel simplify their usage.
3. Remember to use current-limiting resistors to prevent damage to the LEDs and to check the forward voltage and current requirements of the LEDs you are using. LEDs are a great starting point for learning about electronic components and programming with Arduino.

Push Buttons: Input buttons for user interaction.

Push buttons are fundamental input components used in Arduino projects to allow user interaction. Here's how you can use push buttons with Arduino:

1. **Basic Push Button:** A simple push button can be used to detect whether it's pressed or not. Connect one terminal of the button to a digital pin on the Arduino and the other terminal to the ground (GND). Use a pull-up or pull-down resistor to ensure stable readings when the button is not pressed.

- **Pull-up Resistor Configuration:**

Connect one button terminal to the digital pin and the other terminal to 5V. Add a resistor (typically 10kΩ) between the button terminal connected to the digital pin and ground. Illustration 1

- **Pull-down Resistor Configuration:**

Connect one button terminal to the digital pin and the other terminal to ground. Add a resistor (typically 10kΩ) between the button terminal connected to the digital pin and 5V. Illustration 2

Here's an example sketch using the pull-up resistor configuration:

INTERNAL PULL-UP RESISTOR CONFIGURATION

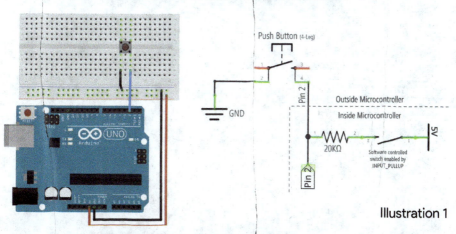

Illustration 1

PULL-DOWN RESISTOR CONFIGURATION

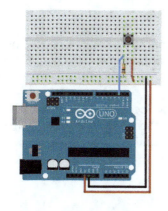

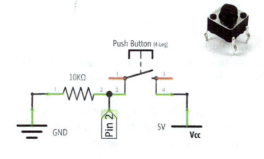

13

Illustration 2

{code example 1}

```
1.   const int buttonPin = 2; // Pin where the button is connected
2.   int buttonState = HIGH; // State of the button (not pressed)
3.   int lastButtonState = HIGH; // Previous state of the button
4.   unsigned long lastDebounceTime = 0; // Time of the last button state change
5.   unsigned long debounceDelay = 50; // Debounce time in milliseconds
6.
7.   void setup() {
8.     pinMode(buttonPin, INPUT_PULLUP); // Set button pin as input with internal pull-up
       resistor
9.     // Other setup code...
10.  }
11.  void loop() {
12.    int reading = digitalRead(buttonPin); // Read the button state
13.    if (reading != lastButtonState) {
14.      lastDebounceTime = millis(); // Record the time of the state change
15.    }
16.    if ((millis() - lastDebounceTime) > debounceDelay) {
17.      // If the button state has been stable for the debounce time
18.      if (reading != buttonState) {
19.        buttonState = reading; // Update button state
20.        if (buttonState == LOW) {
21.          // Button is pressed
22.          // Perform actions here...
23.        }
24.      }
25.    }
26.
27.    lastButtonState = reading; // Update the last button state
28.    // Other loop code...
29.  }
```

In this example, the debounce mechanism helps to prevent false readings caused by mechanical noise when the button is pressed or released. The button's state change is only considered after a stable period of time.

Remember to adjust the pin number and debounce delay according to your setup. Using buttons with Arduino is a great way to enable user interaction in your projects, from simple actions like turning on LEDs to more complex functionalities.

Potentiometers: Adjustable resistors for analog input.

Potentiometers (or pots) are analog input devices that allow users to provide variable input to an Arduino project. They're often used to control things like volume, brightness, or motor speed. Here's how you can use potentiometers with Arduino:

Basic Potentiometer Setup: A potentiometer has three terminals - the two outer ones are the fixed resistors, and the middle one is the variable tap. Connect one outer terminal to 5V and the other to ground. Connect the middle terminal to an analog input pin on the Arduino. Illustration 1

Reading Potentiometer Values: Potentiometers create a voltage divider circuit. The analogRead() function reads the voltage at the analog pin and returns a value between 0 and 1023 (for a 10-bit ADC). You can map this value to the desired range of values (e.g., 0-255 for analogWrite()). Illustration 2

Here's an example sketch

{code example 1}

Illustration 1

```
1.   const int potPin = A0; // Analog pin
     where the potentiometer is connect-
     ed
2.   int potValue = 0; // Variable to store
     potentiometer value
3.
4.   void setup() {
5.     // No need to set up anything specif-
     ic for the potentiometer
6.     // Other setup code...
7.   }
8.
9.   void loop() {
10.    potValue = analogRead(potPin); //
     Read the potentiometer value
11.    int mappedValue = map(potValue, 0,
     1023, 0, 255); // Map value to 0-255
     range
12.
13.    // Use the mapped value for further
     actions, e.g., controlling LED bright-
     ness
14.    analogWrite(LED_PIN, mappedVal-
     ue);
15.
16.    // Other loop code...
17.  }
```

Illustration 2

15

In this example, the potentiometer's value is read using analogRead(), then mapped to a range suitable for analogWrite(), which is commonly used to control the brightness of LEDs.

Using Multiple Potentiometers: You can connect multiple potentiometers to different analog input pins and read their values independently.

{code example 2}

```
1.   const int potPin1 = A0;
2.   const int potPin2 = A1;
3.
4.   int potValue1 = 0;
5.   int potValue2 = 0;
6.
7.   void setup() {
8.     // Other setup code...
9.   }
10.
11.  void loop() {
12.    potValue1 = analogRead(potPin1);
13.    potValue2 = analogRead(potPin2);
14.
15.    int mappedValue1 = map(potValue1, 0, 1023, 0, 255);
16.    int mappedValue2 = map(potValue2, 0, 1023, 0, 255);
17.
18.    // Use the mapped values for different actions
19.    analogWrite(LED_PIN1, mappedValue1);
20.    analogWrite(LED_PIN2, mappedValue2);
21.
22.    // Other loop code...
23.  }
24.
```

By using potentiometers, you can create interactive elements in your projects that allow users to adjust parameters in real-time. This makes your projects more engaging and flexible.

Variable Resistor (Rheostat)

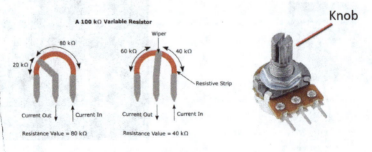

Servo Motors: Small motors for precise control.

Servo motors are widely used in Arduino projects for their precise control over rotation or position. They are commonly used in robotics, automation, and other applications where accurate control of angular position is required. Here's how you can use servo motors with Arduino:

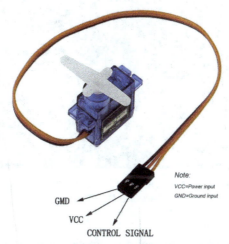

GMD

VCC

CONTROL SIGNAL

Note:
VCC=Power input
GND=Ground input

Basic Servo Motor Setup: Servo motors have three wires - power (usually red), ground (usually black or brown), and control signal (usually yellow or orange). Connect the power wire to a suitable power source (typically 4.8V to 6V for most hobby servos), the ground wire to the ground of the power source, and the control signal wire to a digital pin on the Arduino.

Servo Library: Arduino provides a built-in Servo library that simplifies servo motor control. You need to include the library at the beginning of your sketch. Code Example 1

{code example 1}

```
1.   #include <Servo.h> // Include the Servo library
2.
3.   const int servoPin = 9; // Digital pin where the servo control signal is connected
4.   Servo myservo; // Create a servo object
5.
6.   void setup() {
7.     myservo.attach(servoPin); // Attach the servo to the specified pin
8.     // Other setup code...
9.   }
10.
11.  void loop() {
12.    // Use the write() function to set the servo angle
13.    myservo.write(90); // Set servo to 90 degrees
14.    delay(1000); // Wait for a second
15.
16.    myservo.write(0); // Set servo to 0 degrees
17.    delay(1000); // Wait for a second
18.  }
```

Controlling Servo Angle: The write() function is used to set the angle of the servo. Most servos have an operating range of around 0 to 180 degrees, though some may have a slightly larger range.

Sweeping Servo: You can create a sweeping motion by gradually changing the servo angle. Code Example 2

{code example 2}

```
1.   #include <Servo.h>
2.
3.   const int servoPin = 9;
4.   Servo myservo;
5.
6.   void setup() {
7.     myservo.attach(servoPin);
8.   }
9.
10.  void loop() {
11.    for (int angle = 0; angle <= 180; angle++) {
12.      myservo.write(angle); // Move servo to the current angle
13.      delay(15); // Small delay for smooth motion
14.    }
15.
16.    for (int angle = 180; angle >= 0; angle−) {
17.      myservo.write(angle);
18.      delay(15);
19.    }
20.  }
```

Using Multiple Servos: You can control multiple servo motors by creating separate Servo objects for each servo and attaching them to different pins. Code Example 3

18

{code example 3}

```
1.   #include <Servo.h>
2.
3.   const int servoPin = 9;
4.   Servo myservo;
5.
6.   void setup() {
7.     myservo.attach(servoPin);
8.   }
9.
10.  void loop() {
11.    for (int angle = 0; angle <= 180; angle++) {
12.      myservo.write(angle); // Move servo to the current angle
13.      delay(15); // Small delay for smooth motion
14.    }
15.
16.    for (int angle = 180; angle >= 0; angle--) {
17.      myservo.write(angle);
18.      delay(15);
19.    }
20. }
```

Using servo motors with Arduino allows you to create intricate motion control mechanisms in your projects. Whether it's opening a door, moving a robotic arm, or controlling camera angles, servos provide precise and controlled movement.

Stepper Motors: Motors that move in discrete steps.

Stepper motors are widely used in Arduino projects when precise control over rotation or linear movement is required. Unlike regular DC motors, stepper motors move in discrete steps, allowing for accurate positioning and control. Here's how you can use stepper motors with Arduino:

Basic Stepper Motor Setup: Stepper motors have multiple coils that are energized in a specific sequence to make the motor move in steps. They come in different types such as Unipolar and Bipolar, and they may have varying numbers of steps per revolution.

Stepper Motor Drivers: Most stepper motors require a specialized stepper motor driver to control them. Common driver chips include the A4988 and DRV8825. These drivers interpret control signals from the Arduino and provide the appropriate current and voltage levels to the motor coils.

Stepper Library: The Arduino provides a Stepper library that simplifies the control of stepper motors. You need to include the library at the beginning of your sketch. Code Example 1

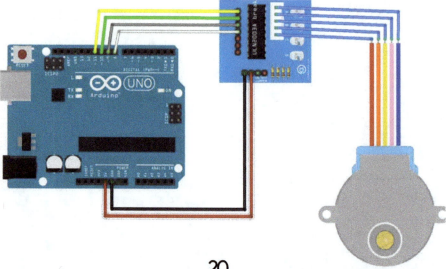

{code example 1}

```
1.   #include <Stepper.h> // Include the Stepper library
2.
3.   // Define the number of steps per revolution for your motor
4.   const int stepsPerRevolution = 200;
5.
6.   // Create a Stepper object
7.   Stepper myStepper(stepsPerRevolution, 8, 9, 10, 11);
8.
9.   void setup() {
10.  // Nothing specific to set up for the stepper motor
11.  }
12.
13.  void loop() {
14.  // Rotate the motor 1 revolution in one direction
15.  myStepper.step(stepsPerRevolution);
16.  delay(1000); // Wait for a second
17.
18.  // Rotate the motor 1 revolution in the opposite direction
19.  myStepper.step(-stepsPerRevolution);
20.  delay(1000);
21.  }
```

Controlling Stepper Movement: The step() function is used to control the movement of the stepper motor. Positive values rotate the motor in one direction, while negative values rotate it in the opposite direction. The actual speed of the rotation depends on the speed set by the driver and the delay between steps in your code.

Microstepping: Some stepper motor drivers support microstepping, which allows for even finer control of the motor's position. Microstepping divides each step into smaller sub-steps, resulting in smoother movement and reduced vibration. The exact steps per revolution may change when using microstepping. Code Example 2

{code example 2}

```
1.   // Example using A4988 driver with 1/16 microstepping
2.   const int stepsPerRevolution = 200 * 16; // Total steps for 1 revolution in 1/16 micro-
     stepping mode
```

Using Multiple Stepper Motors: You can control multiple stepper motors by creating separate Stepper objects and providing the appropriate pin connections.
Code Example 3

{code example 3}

```
1.   #include <Stepper.h>
2.
3.   const int stepsPerRevolution = 200;
4.   Stepper stepper1(stepsPerRevolution, 8, 9, 10, 11);
5.   Stepper stepper2(stepsPerRevolution, 4, 5, 6, 7);
6.
7.   void setup() {
8.     // Nothing specific to set up for the stepper motors
9.   }
10.
11.  void loop() {
12.    stepper1.step(stepsPerRevolution);
13.    stepper2.step(-stepsPerRevolution);
14.    delay(1000);
15.  }
```

Stepper motors are excellent for applications requiring precise control, such as CNC machines, 3D printers, robotic arms, and more. The Arduino Stepper library simplifies their control, making it relatively straightforward to incorporate them into your projects.

DC Motors: Simple motors for basic motion.

DC (Direct Current) motors are common components used for basic motion control in Arduino projects. They're widely used in various applications, from simple robots to remote-controlled cars. Here's how you can use DC motors with Arduino:

Basic DC Motor Setup: DC motors typically have two terminals - positive and negative. They can be powered using a suitable voltage source (such as a battery) and controlled using an Arduino to control the direction and speed of rotation.

Connecting the Motor: Connect one terminal of the motor to one of the motor driver outputs and the other terminal to the other output. Connect the remaining two driver outputs to the Arduino pins that control the motor direction.

Controlling DC Motors: The motor driver allows you to control the motor's direction and speed using digital pins on the Arduino. You'll set the digital pins to HIGH or LOW to control the motor's rotation direction and use analogWrite() to control the speed using PWM (Pulse Width Modulation).

Here's a simple example using the L293D motor driver:

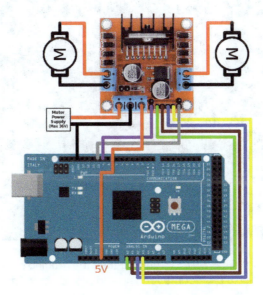

{code example 1}

```
1.  const int motor1EN = 10; // Enable pin for motor 1
2.  const int motor1A = 8;  // Control pin A for motor 1
3.  const int motor1B = 9;  // Control pin B for motor 1
4.  void setup() {
5.    pinMode(motor1EN, OUTPUT);
6.    pinMode(motor1A, OUTPUT);
7.    pinMode(motor1B, OUTPUT);
8.  }
9.  void loop() {
10.   digitalWrite(motor1A, HIGH); // Set direction A for motor 1
11.   digitalWrite(motor1B, LOW); // Set direction B for motor 1
12.   analogWrite(motor1EN, 255); // Set speed of motor 1 (0-255)
13.   delay(2000); // Run for 2 seconds
14.
15.   digitalWrite(motor1A, LOW); // Set direction A for motor 1
16.   digitalWrite(motor1B, HIGH); // Set direction B for motor 1
17.   analogWrite(motor1EN, 128); // Set speed of motor 1 (0-255)
18.   delay(2000);
19.   digitalWrite(motor1EN, LOW); // Turn off motor 1
20.   delay(1000);
21. }
```

Using Multiple DC Motors: For controlling multiple DC motors, you can extend the set-up to include additional motor drivers and pins.

{code example 2}

```
1.  const int motor1EN = 10;
2.  const int motor1A = 8;
3.  const int motor1B = 9;
4.  const int motor2EN = 5; // Enable pin for motor 2
5.  const int motor2A = 6;  // Control pin A for motor 2
6.  const int motor2B = 7;  // Control pin B for motor 2
7.
8.  void setup() {
9.    pinMode(motor1EN, OUTPUT);
10.   pinMode(motor1A, OUTPUT);
11.   pinMode(motor1B, OUTPUT);
12.
13.   pinMode(motor2EN, OUTPUT);
14.   pinMode(motor2A, OUTPUT);
15.   pinMode(motor2B, OUTPUT);
16. }
17. void loop() {
18.   // Control motor 1 and motor 2 independently
19.   // Similar to the single motor example
20. }
21.
```

Remember to connect the power supply for the motor driver separately from the Arduino's power. DC motors can draw more current than the Arduino can handle, so using a motor driver is essential to protect the Arduino and provide efficient control.

Ultrasonic Sensors: Measures distance using sound waves.

Ultrasonic sensors are widely used in Arduino projects for measuring distance without physical contact. They work by emitting a sound wave and measuring the time it takes for the wave to bounce back after hitting an object. Here's how you can use ultrasonic sensors with Arduino:

Basic Ultrasonic Sensor Setup: Ultrasonic sensors have two main components: a transmitter that sends out sound waves and a receiver that listens for the echo. To use an ultrasonic sensor, you typically need to connect four pins: Vcc (power), GND (ground), Trig (trigger), and Echo (echo/receive).

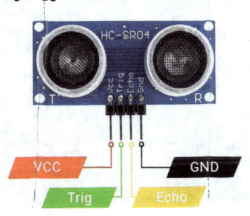

Ultrasonic Library: Although it's possible to work with ultrasonic sensors using basic Arduino functions, there are libraries available that simplify the process. The "NewPing" library is a popular choice.

Using the NewPing Library:

- First, you need to install the NewPing library through the Arduino IDE: Sketch > Include Library > Manage Libraries, then search for "NewPing" and install it.
- Once installed, you can use the library to easily read distance measurements from the ultrasonic sensor.

Here's an example using the NewPing library:

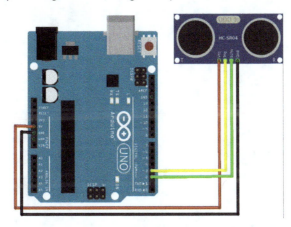

{code example 1}

```
1.   #include <NewPing.h> // Include the NewPing library
2.
3.   #define TRIGGER_PIN 12 // Arduino pin connected to the trigger pin of the sensor
4.   #define ECHO_PIN 11   // Arduino pin connected to the echo pin of the sensor
5.   #define MAX_DISTANCE 200 // Maximum distance to measure in centimeters
6.
7.   NewPing sonar(TRIGGER_PIN, ECHO_PIN, MAX_DISTANCE); // Create a NewPing
     object
8.
9.   void setup() {
10.   Serial.begin(9600); // Start serial communication
11.  }
12.
13.  void loop() {
14.   delay(50); // Delay for stability
15.
16.   unsigned int distance = sonar.ping_cm(); // Measure distance in centimeters
17.
18.   Serial.print("Distance: ");
19.   Serial.print(distance);
20.   Serial.println(" cm");
21.
22.   // Other loop code...
23. }
```

- In this example, the NewPing library is used to create an instance of the New-Ping class. The ping_cm() function returns the distance in centimeters.
- **Multiple Ultrasonic Sensors:** You can use multiple ultrasonic sensors by creating separate 'NewPing' objects for each sensor.

Here's an example using the NewPing library:

{code example 2}

```
1.  #include <NewPing.h>
2.
3.  #define TRIGGER_PIN1 12
4.  #define ECHO_PIN1 11
5.  #define TRIGGER_PIN2 8
6.  #define ECHO_PIN2 7
7.  #define MAX_DISTANCE 200
8.
9.  NewPing sonar1(TRIGGER_PIN1, ECHO_PIN1, MAX_DISTANCE);
10. NewPing sonar2(TRIGGER_PIN2, ECHO_PIN2, MAX_DISTANCE);
11.
12. void setup() {
13.   Serial.begin(9600);
14. }
15.
16. void loop() {
17.   unsigned int distance1 = sonar1.ping_cm();
18.   unsigned int distance2 = sonar2.ping_cm();
19.
20.   Serial.print("Distance Sensor 1: ");
21.   Serial.print(distance1);
22.   Serial.println(" cm");
23.
24.   Serial.print("Distance Sensor 2: ");
25.   Serial.print(distance2);
26.   Serial.println(" cm");
27.
28.   // Other loop code...
29. }
```

Ultrasonic sensors are commonly used for object detection, obstacle avoidance, and distance measurement in robotics and automation projects. The NewPing library makes working with ultrasonic sensors a lot easier and provides accurate distance readings.

IR Sensors: Infrared sensors for detecting objects

IR (Infrared) sensors are commonly used in Arduino projects to detect the presence or absence of objects based on their reflection of infrared light. They are often used for proximity sensing, line following, and object detection. Here's how you can use IR sensors with Arduino:

Basic IR Sensor Setup: IR sensors consist of an IR emitter (LED) and a photodiode that detects reflected IR light. When an object is close, the photodiode receives more reflected light. Depending on the type of IR sensor, you might have analog or digital output.

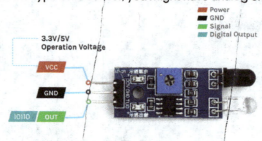

Analog IR Sensors: These sensors provide analog voltage values that correspond to the intensity of the reflected IR light. You can connect the sensor to an analog pin on the Arduino.

Here's an example using an analog IR sensor:

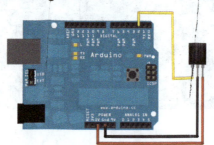

{code example 1}

```
1.   const int irSensorPin = 2; // Digital pin where the IR sensor is connected
2.
3.   void setup() {
4.     pinMode(irSensorPin, INPUT); // Set the pin as input
5.     Serial.begin(9600);
6.   }
7.   void loop() {
8.     int sensorValue = digitalRead(irSensorPin); // Read digital value
9.     if (sensorValue == HIGH) {
10.      Serial.println("Object Detected");
11.    } else {
12.      Serial.println("No Object Detected");
13.    }
14.    // Other loop code...
15.  }
```

Digital IR Sensors: Digital IR sensors have a built-in comparator that outputs a digital signal (HIGH or LOW) based on a threshold value. These sensors are often used for obstacle detection.

Here's an example using a digital IR sensor:

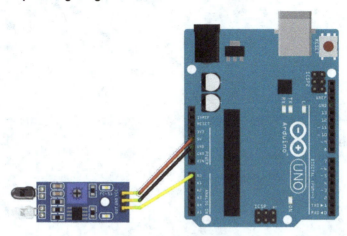

{code example 2}

```
1.   const int irSensorPin = 2; // Digital pin where the IR sensor is connected
2.
3.   void setup() {
4.     pinMode(irSensorPin, INPUT); // Set the pin as input
5.     Serial.begin(9600);
6.   }
7.
8.   void loop() {
9.     int sensorValue = digitalRead(irSensorPin); // Read digital value
10.    if (sensorValue == HIGH) {
11.      Serial.println("Object Detected");
12.    } else {
13.      Serial.println("No Object Detected");
14.    }
15.
16.    // Other loop code...
17.  }
```

Multiple IR Sensors: You can use multiple IR sensors by connecting them to different pins and reading their values individually

{code example 3}

```
1.   const int irSensorPin1 = 2;
2.   const int irSensorPin2 = 3;
3.
4.   void setup() {
5.     pinMode(irSensorPin1, INPUT);
6.     pinMode(irSensorPin2, INPUT);
7.     Serial.begin(9600);
8.   }
9.
10.  void loop() {
11.    int sensorValue1 = digitalRead(irSensorPin1);
12.    int sensorValue2 = digitalRead(irSensorPin2);
13.
14.    if (sensorValue1 == HIGH) {
15.      Serial.println("Object Detected by Sensor 1");
16.    }
17.    if (sensorValue2 == HIGH) {
18.      Serial.println("Object Detected by Sensor 2");
19.    }
20.
21.    // Other loop code...
22.  }
23.
```

IR sensors are commonly used for various applications like obstacle avoidance in robots, line following in line follower robots, and presence detection in home automation systems. They are versatile sensors that provide valuable input for decision-making in your projects.

Temperature Sensors: For Measuring temperature Parameters.

Temperature sensors are essential components in Arduino projects for measuring ambient or object temperatures. They allow you to monitor and respond to temperature changes, making them useful for various applications like weather stations, home automation, and temperature-sensitive projects. Here's how you can use temperature sensors with Arduino:

Basic Temperature Sensor Setup: There are various types of temperature sensors available, such as the DHT11, DHT22 (also known as AM2302), DS18B20, and LM35. Each sensor has its own wiring and coding requirements.

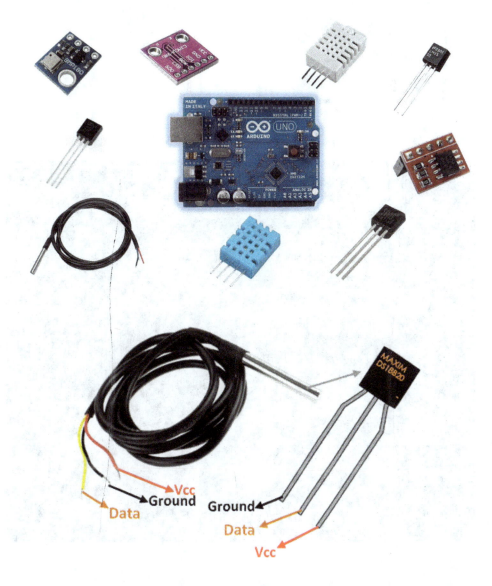

DHT11/DHT22 (AM2302): These are digital temperature and humidity sensors that communicate over a single wire using a specific protocol. You can use the "DHT" library to read their values.

Here's an example using the DHT22 sensor:

{code example 1}

```
1.   #include <DHT.h> // Include the DHT library
2.
3.   #define DHTPIN 2     // Digital pin where the DHT sensor is connected
4.   #define DHTTYPE DHT22 // DHT22 sensor type
5.
6.   DHT dht(DHTPIN, DHTTYPE); // Create a DHT object
7.
8.   void setup() {
9.     Serial.begin(9600); // Start serial communication
10.   dht.begin(); // Initialize the DHT sensor
11.   }
12.
13.  void loop() {
14.    float temperature = dht.readTemperature(); // Read temperature in Celsius
15.    float humidity = dht.readHumidity(); // Read humidity
16.
17.    Serial.print("Temperature: ");
18.    Serial.print(temperature);
19.    Serial.print(" °C, Humidity: ");
20.    Serial.print(humidity);
21.    Serial.println(" %");
22.
23.    // Other loop code...
24.    delay(2000); // Delay to avoid frequent readings
25.  }
```

DS18B20: This is a digital temperature sensor with a unique address for each sensor on the same bus. You'll need the "OneWire" and "DallasTemperature" libraries for this sensor.

Here's an example using the DS18B20 sensor:

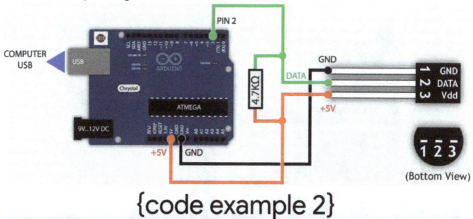

{code example 2}

```
1.  #include <OneWire.h>
2.  #include <DallasTemperature.h>
3.
4.  #define ONE_WIRE_BUS 2 // Digital pin where the DS18B20 is connected
5.
6.  OneWire oneWire(ONE_WIRE_BUS);
7.  DallasTemperature sensors(&oneWire);
8.
9.  void setup() {
10.   Serial.begin(9600);
11.   sensors.begin(); // Initialize the DallasTemperature library
12. }
13.
14. void loop() {
15.   sensors.requestTemperatures(); // Send the command to get temperature readings
16.
17.   float temperature = sensors.getTempCByIndex(0); // Read temperature in Celsius
18.
19.   Serial.print("Temperature: ");
20.   Serial.print(temperature);
21.   Serial.println(" °C");
22.
23.   // Other loop code...
24.   delay(2000);
25. }
```

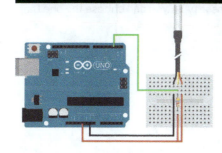

LM35: The LM35 is an analog temperature sensor that provides an analog voltage proportional to the temperature. You can convert the analog reading to Celsius using appropriate calculations.

Here's an example using the LM35 sensor:

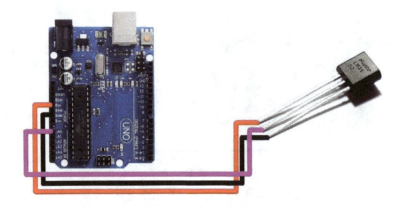

{code example 3}

```
1.    const int lm35Pin = A0; // Analog pin where the LM35 sensor is connected
2.
3.    void setup() {
4.      Serial.begin(9600);
5.    }
6.
7.    void loop() {
8.      int rawValue = analogRead(lm35Pin); // Read analog value
9.
10.     // Convert the analog value to temperature in Celsius
11.     float temperature = (rawValue * 5.0 / 1023.0 - 0.5) * 100.0;
12.
13.     Serial.print("Temperature: ");
14.     Serial.print(temperature);
15.     Serial.println(" °C");
16.
17.     // Other loop code
18.     delay(2000);
19.   }
```

Temperature sensors provide crucial data for monitoring and controlling environmental conditions in your projects. Depending on the sensor type, you can choose the one that best suits your accuracy requirements and interface preferences.

Humidity Sensors: Measures humidity in the air.

Humidity sensors are essential components in many Arduino projects that involve monitoring and controlling environmental conditions. These sensors measure the amount of moisture present in the air, providing valuable information for applications like weather monitoring, plant care, and home automation. Here's how you can use humidity sensors with Arduino:

Basic Humidity Sensor Setup: There are various types of humidity sensors available, such as the DHT11, DHT22 (AM2302), and SHT series. These sensors can provide combined temperature and humidity measurements.

DHT11/DHT22 (AM2302): These are digital humidity and temperature sensors that communicate over a single wire using a specific protocol. You can use the "DHT" library to read their values.

Here's an example using the DHT22 sensor to measure humidity:s.

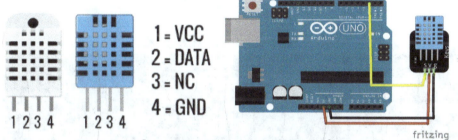

1 = VCC
2 = DATA
3 = NC
4 = GND

1 2 3 4   1 2 3 4

fritzing

{code example 1}

```
1.   #include <DHT.h> // Include the DHT library
2.
3.   #define DHTPIN 2     // Digital pin where the DHT sensor is connected
4.   #define DHTTYPE DHT22  // DHT22 sensor type
5.
6.   DHT dht(DHTPIN, DHTTYPE); // Create a DHT object
7.
8.   void setup() {
9.     Serial.begin(9600); // Start serial communication
10.   dht.begin(); // Initialize the DHT sensor
11.  }
12.
13.  void loop() {
14.    float humidity = dht.readHumidity(); // Read humidity
15.
16.    Serial.print("Humidity: ");
17.    Serial.print(humidity);
18.    Serial.println(" %");
19.
20.    // Other loop code...
21.    delay(2000); // Delay to avoid frequent readings
22. }
```

SHT Series: These sensors are known for their accuracy and stability. They communicate using the I2C protocol and provide temperature and humidity values.

Here's an example using the SHT sensor with the "Adafruit_SHT31" library:

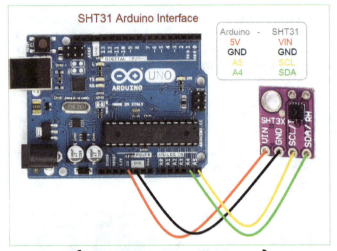

{code example 2}

```
1.  #include <Wire.h>
2.  #include <Adafruit_SHT31.h>
3.
4.  Adafruit_SHT31 sht31 = Adafruit_SHT31();
5.
6.  void setup() {
7.    Serial.begin(9600);
8.    if (!sht31.begin(0x44)) { // Set the I2C address
9.      Serial.println("Couldn't find SHT31");
10.     while (1);
11.   }
12. }
13.
14. void loop() {
15.   float humidity = sht31.readHumidity();
16.
17.   Serial.print("Humidity; ");
18.   Serial.print(humidity);
19.   Serial.println(" %");
20.
21.   // Other loop code...
22.   delay(2000);
23. }
24.
```

Humidity sensors are indispensable for maintaining optimal conditions in various scenarios. Depending on the accuracy and features you require, you can choose the appropriate humidity sensor for your project.

Light Sensors: Measures ambient light intensity.

Light sensors are commonly used in Arduino projects to measure the ambient light intensity in their surroundings. These sensors help you detect changes in light conditions, enabling applications like automatic lighting, smart energy management, and more. Here's how you can use light sensors with Arduino:

Basic Light Sensor Setup: There are different types of light sensors available, such as LDRs (Light Dependent Resistors) and photodiodes. LDRs are simple and widely used. Their resistance changes with light intensity.

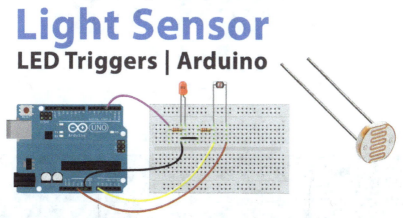

Analog Light Sensor (LDR): LDRs are analog sensors that change their resistance based on the amount of light they receive. You can connect them to an analog pin on the Arduino.

Here's an example using an LDR to measure light intensity:

{code example 1}

```
1.   const int ldrPin = A0; // Analog pin where the LDR is connected
2.
3.   void setup() {
4.     Serial.begin(9600); // Start serial communication
5.   }
6.
7.   void loop() {
8.     int sensorValue = analogRead(ldrPin); // Read analog value
9.
10.    Serial.print("Light Intensity: ");
11.    Serial.println(sensorValue);
12.
13.    // Add your logic here based on sensor value
14.    // For example, if (sensorValue < threshold), it's dark
15.
16.    delay(1000); // Delay to avoid frequent readings
17.  }
```

Digital Light Sensor (Photodiode) TEMT6000: Photodiodes are light-sensitive semi-conductor devices that generate a digital signal based on light intensity. You can use a voltage divider circuit to interface them with Arduino's digital pins.
Here's an example using a photodiode to measure light intensity:

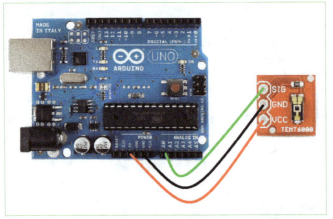

{code example 2}

```
1.   const int photodiodePin = 2; // Digital pin where the photodiode is connected
2.
3.   void setup() {
4.     pinMode(photodiodePin, INPUT); // Set the pin as input
5.     Serial.begin(9600);
6.   }
7.
8.   void loop() {
9.     int sensorValue = digitalRead(photodiodePin); // Read digital value
10.
11.    if (sensorValue == HIGH) {
12.      Serial.println("Light Detected");
13.    } else {
14.      Serial.println("Dark");
15.    }
16.
17.    // Other loop code...
18.    delay(1000);
19.  }
20.
```

Using a Light Sensor Module: You can also use light sensor modules that often include additional components like comparators for digital outputs. These modules make it easier to interface with the Arduino.
Remember to calibrate the sensor according to your environment and requirements.
Light sensors can help create energy-efficient systems and provide useful information about lighting conditions in your projects.

sound sensors, also known as sound detection modules or microphones

Sound sensors, also known as sound detection modules or microphones, are commonly used in Arduino projects to measure sound levels and detect sound events. These sensors can be used for applications like noise monitoring, sound-activated triggers, and audio-based projects. Here's how you can use sound sensors with Arduino:

Basic Sound Sensor Setup: Sound sensors typically contain a microphone element that converts sound waves into electrical signals. There are both analog and digital sound sensors available.

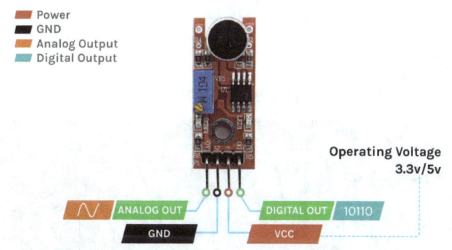

Analog Sound Sensor: Analog sound sensors output a voltage that corresponds to the sound intensity they detect. You can connect them to an analog pin on the Arduino.

Here's an example using an analog sound sensor to measure sound intensity:

{code example 1}

```
1.   const int soundSensorPin = A0; // Analog pin where the sound sensor is connected
2.
3.   void setup() {
4.     Serial.begin(9600); // Start serial communication
5.   }
6.
7.   void loop() {
8.     int sensorValue = analogRead(soundSensorPin); // Read analog value
9.
10.    Serial.print("Sound Intensity: ");
11.    Serial.println(sensorValue);
12.
13.    // Add your logic here based on sensor value
14.    // For example, if (sensorValue > threshold), sound detected
15.
16.    delay(1000); // Delay to avoid frequent readings
17.  }
```

Digital Sound Sensor: Digital sound sensors provide a simple digital output that changes when a sound is detected above a certain threshold. They often have built-in threshold circuitry.

Here's an example using a digital sound sensor:

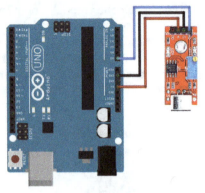

{code example 2}

```
1.    const int soundSensorPin = 2; // Digital pin where the sound sensor is connected
2.
3.    void setup() {
4.      pinMode(soundSensorPin, INPUT); // Set the pin as input
5.      Serial.begin(9600);
6.    }
7.
8.    void loop() {
9.      int sensorValue = digitalRead(soundSensorPin); // Read digital value
10.
11.     if (sensorValue == HIGH) {
12.       Serial.println("Sound Detected");
13.     } else {
14.       Serial.println("No Sound");
15.     }
16.
17.     // Other loop code...
18.     delay(1000);
19.  }
20.
```

Using a Sound Sensor Module: Sound sensor modules often include additional components like amplifiers and comparators for more accurate sound detection. These modules make it easier to interface with the Arduino.

Sound sensors are useful for projects involving sound-based triggers, noise measurement, voice recognition, and more. Depending on your specific use case, you can choose between analog and digital sound sensors or sound sensor modules to achieve the desired functionality.

Gas Sensors: Detects various gases in the environment

Gas sensors are important components in many Arduino projects that involve monitoring and detecting various gases in the environment. These sensors can be used for applications like air quality monitoring, gas leakage detection, and more. Here's how you can use gas sensors with Arduino:

Basic Gas Sensor Setup: Gas sensors are available for various gases, such as carbon dioxide (CO2), carbon monoxide (CO), methane (CH4), and volatile organic compounds (VOCs). Different gas sensors require different interfacing methods and libraries.

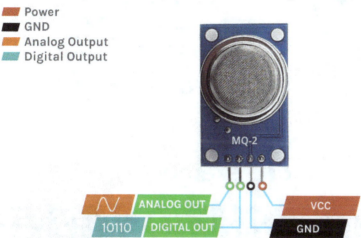

- Power
- GND
- Analog Output
- Digital Output

MQ Series Gas Sensors: The MQ series is a popular family of gas sensors that can detect a wide range of gases. Each sensor in the MQ series is designed for a specific gas and has a unique sensitivity curve. You will need to consult the datasheet for your specific MQ sensor to determine the correct connections and sensitivity.

Here's a generic example of using an MQ series gas sensor:

{code example 1}

```
1.  const int gasSensorPin = A0; // Analog pin where the gas sensor is connected
2.
3.  void setup() {
4.    Serial.begin(9600); // Start serial communication
5.  }
6.
7.  void loop() {
8.    int sensorValue = analogRead(gasSensorPin); // Read analog value
9.
10.   Serial.print("Gas Sensor Value: ");
11.   Serial.println(sensorValue);
12.
13.   // Add your logic here based on sensor value
14.   // For example, if (sensorValue > threshold), gas detected
15.
16.   delay(1000); // Delay to avoid frequent readings
17. }
```

Using Gas Sensor Modules: For more advanced gas sensing applications, you can use gas sensor modules that often include built-in amplifiers and pre-processing circuitry. These modules simplify the interface with the Arduino.
Here's an example using a gas sensor module:

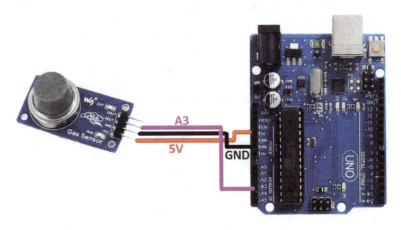

{code example 2}

```
1.   const int gasSensorPin = 2; // Digital pin where the gas sensor module is connected
2.
3.   void setup() {
4.     pinMode(gasSensorPin, INPUT); // Set the pin as input
5.     Serial.begin(9600);
6.   }
7.
8.   void loop() {
9.     int sensorValue = digitalRead(gasSensorPin); // Read digital value
10.
11.    if (sensorValue == HIGH) {
12.      Serial.println("Gas Detected");
13.    } else {
14.      Serial.println("No Gas Detected");
15.    }
16.
17.    // Other loop code...
18.    delay(1000);
19.  }
```

Specific Gas Sensors: Some gas sensors are designed for specific gases like CO2 or methane. These sensors often come with dedicated libraries and communication protocols for accurate measurement and control.
Gas sensors are vital for ensuring safety and monitoring air quality in various environments. Depending on your specific gas detection requirements, you can choose the appropriate gas sensor and interfacing method for your Arduino project.

Accelerometers: Measures acceleration.

Accelerometers are sensors that measure acceleration, typically in three axes (X, Y, and Z). They are widely used in Arduino projects for tasks like motion detection, orientation sensing, and gesture recognition. Here's how you can use accelerometers with Arduino:

Basic Accelerometer Setup: Accelerometers come in various forms, including analog and digital sensors. One common digital accelerometer is the MPU-6050, which combines an accelerometer and a gyroscope in one module.

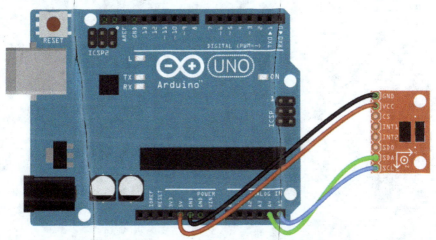

MPU-6050 Digital Accelerometer/Gyroscope: To use the MPU-6050 with Arduino, you'll need to install the "Wire" library, which is used for I2C communication.

Here's an example using the MPU-6050 to read accelerometer data:

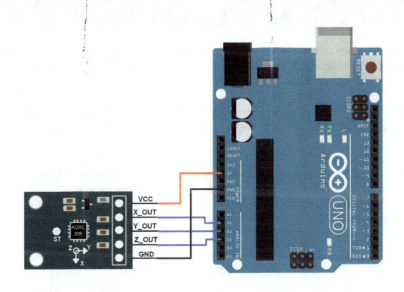

{code example 1}

```
1.  #include <Wire.h>
2.  #include <MPU6050.h>
3.
4.  MPU6050 mpu;
5.
6.  void setup() {
7.    Serial.begin(9600);
8.    Wire.begin();
9.    mpu.initialize(); // Initialize the MPU-6050
10.
11.   // Optionally, set gyroscope offsets if needed
12.   // mpu.setXGyroOffset(0);
13.   // mpu.setYGyroOffset(0);
14.   // mpu.setZGyroOffset(0);
15. }
16.
17. void loop() {
18.   // Read accelerometer data
19.   int16_t ax, ay, az;
20.   mpu.getAcceleration(&ax, &ay, &az);
21.
22.   Serial.print("Acceleration (XYZ): ");
23.   Serial.print(ax);
24.   Serial.print(", ");
25.   Serial.print(ay);
26.   Serial.print(", ");
27.   Serial.println(az);
28.
29.   // Other loop code...
30.   delay(1000);
31. }
```

Calibration: It's often necessary to calibrate the accelerometer to obtain accurate readings. This can involve setting offsets or scaling factors. The specific calibration procedure depends on the accelerometer model you are using.

Other Accelerometer Models: If you're using a different accelerometer model, you'll need to check the datasheet and any available libraries to understand how to interface with it.

Accelerometers are commonly used in projects such as gesture-controlled devices, wearable technology, vehicle tracking, and many more. They provide valuable information about an object's acceleration, making them versatile sensors for motion-related applications.

Gyroscope Sensors: Measures orientation and rotation.

Gyroscope sensors measure orientation and angular velocity, helping you determine the rotational movement of an object. They are commonly used in Arduino projects for applications like balancing robots, motion sensing, and tracking orientation changes. Here's how you can use gyroscope sensors with Arduino:

Basic Gyroscope Sensor Setup: Gyroscope sensors come in various forms, including digital sensors like the MPU-6050 and MPU-9250. These sensors often combine both accelerometer and gyroscope capabilities in a single module.

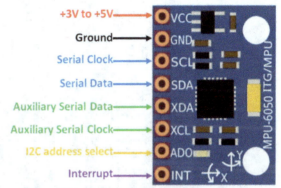

MPU-6050 Digital Gyroscope/Accelerometer: To use the MPU-6050 with Arduino, you'll need to install the "Wire" library for I2C communication, and you can use the "MPU6050" library for simplified interaction.

Here's an example using the MPU-6050 to read gyroscope data:

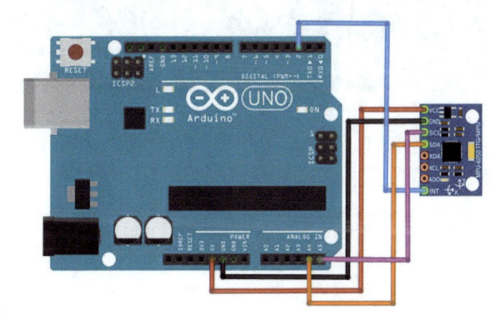

{code example 1}

```
1.   #include <Wire.h>
2.   #include <MPU6050.h>
3.
4.   MPU6050 mpu;
5.
6.   void setup() {
7.     Serial.begin(9600);
8.     Wire.begin();
9.     mpu.initialize(); // Initialize the MPU-6050
10.
11.    // Optionally, set accelerometer and gyroscope offsets if needed
12.    // mpu.setXGyroOffset(0);
13.    // mpu.setYGyroOffset(0);
14.    // mpu.setZGyroOffset(0);
15.    // mpu.setXAccelOffset(0);
16.    // mpu.setYAccelOffset(0);
17.    // mpu.setZAccelOffset(0);
18.  }
19.
20.  void loop() {
21.    // Read gyroscope data
22.    int16_t gx, gy, gz;
23.    mpu.getRotation(&gx, &gy, &gz);
24.
25.    Serial.print("Gyroscope (XYZ): ");
26.    Serial.print(gx);
27.    Serial.print(", ");
28.    Serial.print(gy);
29.    Serial.print(", ");
30.    Serial.println(gz);
31.
32.    // Other loop code...
33.    delay(1000);
34.  }
```

Calibration: Gyroscope sensors often require calibration to obtain accurate readings. Calibration involves setting offsets or scaling factors to correct for biases in the sensor's data. The calibration process can vary based on the sensor model you're using.

Other Gyroscope Models: If you're using a different gyroscope sensor model, consult the datasheet and any available libraries to understand how to interface with it.

Gyroscope sensors provide information about an object's rotational movement and are essential for projects that involve tracking orientation and controlling devices based on angular velocity.

Compass Modules: Measures direction using magnetism.

Compass modules, also known as magnetometers, are sensors that measure the Earth's magnetic field, allowing you to determine direction or orientation. They are commonly used in Arduino projects for tasks like building compasses, tracking heading angles, and navigation applications. Here's how you can use compass modules with Arduino:

Basic Compass Module Setup: Compass modules can be either digital or analog, but digital modules like the HMC5883L and QMC5883L are popular because they provide accurate and calibrated data.

HMC5883L Digital Compass Module: To use the HMC5883L with Arduino, you can use the "Adafruit_Sensor" and "Adafruit_HMC5883_Unified" libraries.

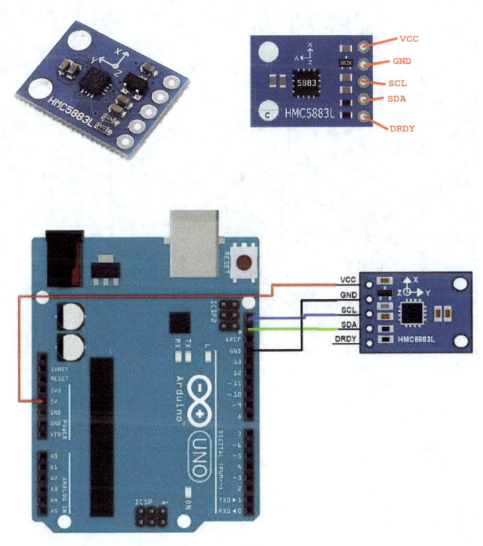

Here's an example using the HMC5883L to read compass data:

{code example 1}

```
1.   #include <Wire.h>
2.   #include <Adafruit_Sensor.h>
3.   #include <Adafruit_HMC5883_U.h>
4.
5.   Adafruit_HMC5883_Unified mag = Adafruit_HMC5883_Unified(12345); // Create a
     magnetometer object
6.
7.   void setup(void) {
8.     Serial.begin(9600);
9.     if (!mag.begin()) {
10.      Serial.println("Could not find a valid HMC5883L sensor, check wiring!");
11.      while (1);
12.    }
13.  }
14.
15.  void loop(void) {
16.    sensors_event_t event;
17.    mag.getEvent(&event);
18.
19.    float heading = atan2(event.magnetic.y, event.magnetic.x);
20.
21.    // Convert radians to degrees for a compass reading between 0 and 360 degrees
22.    if (heading < 0) {
23.      heading += 2 * PI;
24.    }
25.
26.    float headingDegrees = heading * 180 / PI;
27.
28.    Serial.print("Compass Heading: ");
29.    Serial.println(headingDegrees);
30.
31.    // Other loop code...
32.    delay(1000);
33.  }
```

Calibration: Compass modules often require calibration to provide accurate heading readings. Calibration involves rotating the module in all directions to map the magnetic field in your environment. This calibration process can vary based on the sensor model and the library you're using.

Other Compass Modules: If you're using a different compass module, consult its datasheet and available libraries to understand how to interface with it.

Compass modules are crucial for projects that involve navigation, direction finding, or orientation control. They provide a way to determine the heading angle relative to the Earth's magnetic field.

RFID Modules: Reads RFID tags for identification.

RFID (Radio-Frequency Identification) modules are widely used in Arduino projects for identifying and tracking objects or individuals by reading RFID tags. These modules enable applications like access control systems, inventory management, and automated identification processes. Here's how you can use RFID modules with Arduino:

Basic RFID Module Setup: RFID modules consist of an RFID reader and RFID tags. Tags can be passive (powered by the reader's signal) or active (with their own power source). The reader emits radio waves, and when a tag comes into the reader's range, it responds with its unique identification information.

MFRC522 RFID Module: One popular RFID module is the MFRC522. You can use the "MFRC522" library to interface with this module.

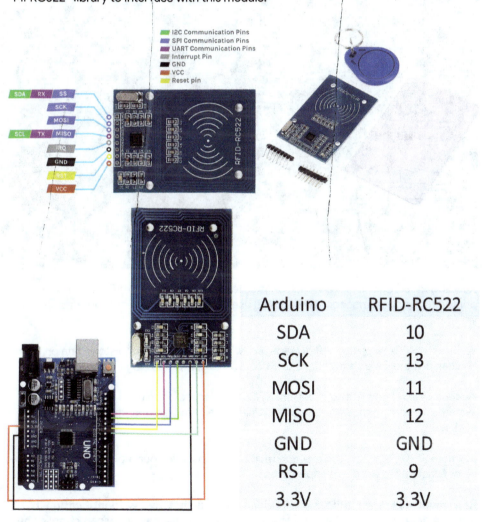

Arduino	RFID-RC522
SDA	10
SCK	13
MOSI	11
MISO	12
GND	GND
RST	9
3.3V	3.3V

Here's an example using the MFRC522 RFID module:

{code example 1}

```
1.  #include <SPI.h>
2.  #include <MFRC522.h>
3.
4.  #define SS_PIN 10   // Define the SS (Slave Select) pin
5.  #define RST_PIN 9   // Define the RST (Reset) pin
6.
7.  MFRC522 mfrc522(SS_PIN, RST_PIN);  // Create an MFRC522 instance
8.
9.  void setup() {
10.   Serial.begin(9600);
11.   SPI.begin();      // Init SPI bus
12.   mfrc522.PCD_Init(); // Init MFRC522 card
13.   Serial.println("RFID Reader Initialized");
14. }
15.
16. void loop() {
17.   // Look for new cards
18.   if (mfrc522.PICC_IsNewCardPresent() && mfrc522.PICC_ReadCardSerial()) {
19.     Serial.print("Card UID: ");
20.     for (byte i = 0; i < mfrc522.uid.size; i++) {
21.       Serial.print(mfrc522.uid.uidByte[i], HEX);
22.       Serial.print(" ");
23.     }
24.     Serial.println();
25.     mfrc522.PICC_HaltA();
26.   }
27.
28.   // Other loop code...
29. }
```

Reading RFID Tags: When an RFID tag is detected, its unique identifier (UID) is read and printed to the serial monitor. You can then use this UID to identify or trigger actions in your project.

Writing to RFID Tags: Some RFID tags are writable, allowing you to store data on them. You can use the library's functions to write data to compatible tags.

Access Control and Authentication: RFID modules are often used for access control systems. You can compare the scanned UID with a database of authorized users to grant access.

Multiple RFID Tags: You can manage multiple RFID tags in your project. The library provides functions to handle multiple cards.

RFID modules are versatile and useful for projects that involve identification, tracking, and access control. Depending on your specific use case, you can choose the appropriate RFID module and library for your Arduino project.

RFID Modules: Reads RFID tags for iden-tification.

Bluetooth modules are widely used in Arduino projects to enable wireless communication between Arduino boards and other devices like smartphones, tablets, or computers. They open up possibilities for remote control, data exchange, and IoT (Internet of Things) applications. Here's how you can use Bluetooth modules with Arduino:

Basic Bluetooth Module Setup: Bluetooth modules come in various versions, such as Bluetooth Classic (like HC-05/HC-06) and Bluetooth Low Energy (BLE, like HM-10/HC-08). You can choose the one that suits your project's requirements.

Bluetooth Classic (HC-05/HC-06): To use Bluetooth Classic modules like HC-05 or HC-06, you'll need to connect them to the Arduino's hardware serial pins (typically pins 0 and 1) for communication.

HC-05 Bluetooth Module

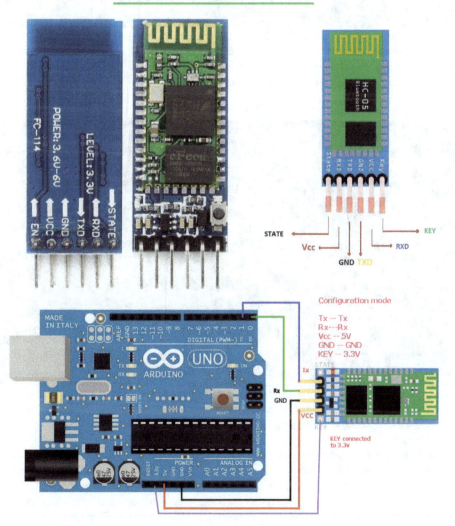

{code example 1}

```
1.   #include <SoftwareSerial.h>
2.   SoftwareSerial bluetooth(2, 3); // RX, TX
3.   void setup() {
4.     Serial.begin(9600);
5.     bluetooth.begin(9600);
6.   }
7.   void loop() {
8.     if (bluetooth.available()) {
9.       char c = bluetooth.read();
10.    Serial.print(c); // Print received data to the serial monitor
11.    }
12.
13.    if (Serial.available()) {
14.      char c = Serial.read();
15.    bluetooth.write(c); // Send data from serial monitor to Bluetooth module
16.    }
17.  }
```

Bluetooth Low Energy (BLE, HM-10/HC-08): BLE modules like HM-10 or HC-08 use a serial communication protocol similar to Bluetooth Classic. You can connect them to software serial pins just like the HC-05/HC-06.

Here's an example using an HM-10 BLE module:

{code example 2}

```
1.   #include <SoftwareSerial.h>
2.   SoftwareSerial bleSerial(2, 3); // RX, TX
3.   void setup() {
4.     Serial.begin(9600);
5.     bleSerial.begin(9600);
6.   }
7.   void loop() {
8.     if (bleSerial.available()) {
9.       char c = bleSerial.read();
10.    Serial.print(c); // Print received data to the serial monitor
11.    }
12.
13.    if (Serial.available()) {
14.      char c = Serial.read();
15.    bleSerial.write(c); // Send data from serial monitor to BLE module
16.    }
17.  }
```

Pairing and Communication: After setting up the hardware and software serial connections, you can pair your Bluetooth module with a smartphone or other Bluetooth-enabled devices. Once paired, you can send and receive data wirelessly between the Arduino and the paired device.

Using Smartphone Apps: To control your Arduino project with a smartphone, you can create a custom mobile app or use existing apps like "Bluetooth Terminal" or "Serial Bluetooth Terminal." These apps allow you to send and receive data over Bluetooth.

Bluetooth modules are versatile and can be used for various applications, including remote control, sensor data monitoring, home automation, and robotics.

Wi-Fi Modules: Adds Wi-Fi communication.

Wi-Fi modules are essential components in Arduino projects that require wireless internet connectivity. These modules enable your Arduino board to connect to Wi-Fi networks, interact with online services, and exchange data with remote servers. Here's how you can use Wi-Fi modules with Arduino:

Basic Wi-Fi Module Setup: There are several Wi-Fi modules available, but one of the most popular choices for Arduino projects is the ESP8266 and its successor, the ESP32. These modules come with built-in Wi-Fi capabilities.

ESP8266 Wi-Fi Module: To use an ESP8266 Wi-Fi module like the ESP-01 or NodeMCU with Arduino, you can use the "ESP8266WiFi" library. Here's a simple example of connecting to a Wi-Fi network and making a GET request to a website:

 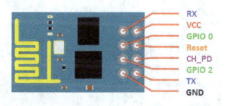

RX
VCC
GPIO 0
Reset
CH_PD
GPIO 2
TX
GND

Introduction to ESP8266

{code example 1}

```
1.  #include <ESP8266WiFi.h>
2.
3.  const char* ssid = "YourNetworkSSID";
4.  const char* password = "YourNetworkPassword";
5.
6.  void setup() {
7.    Serial.begin(115200);
8.    WiFi.begin(ssid, password);
9.
10.   while (WiFi.status() != WL_CONNECTED) {
11.     delay(1000);
12.     Serial.println("Connecting to WiFi...");
13.   }
14.
15.   Serial.println("Connected to WiFi");
16. }
17.
18. void loop() {
19.   // Your Wi-Fi-enabled Arduino code here...
20. }
```

ESP32 Wi-Fi Module: The ESP32 offers more advanced capabilities compared to the ESP8266. You can use the "WiFi.h" library for Wi-Fi communication on the ESP32. Here's a basic example:

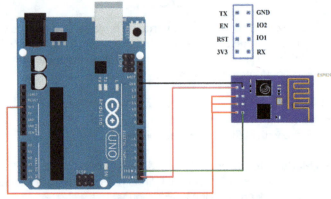

{code example 2}

```
1.   #include <WiFi.h>
2.
3.   const char* ssid = "YourNetworkSSID";
4.   const char* password = "YourNetworkPassword";
5.
6.   void setup() {
7.     Serial.begin(115200);
8.     WiFi.begin(ssid, password);
9.
10.    while (WiFi.status() != WL_CONNECTED) {
11.      delay(1000);
12.      Serial.println("Connecting to WiFi...");
13.    }
14.
15.    Serial.println("Connected to WiFi");
16. }
17.
18. void loop() {
19.    // Your Wi-Fi-enabled Arduino code here...
20. }
```

Web Server and Client: Wi-Fi modules can be used to create web servers, web clients, and IoT devices that interact with web services. You can send HTTP requests, retrieve data, and host web pages directly from your Arduino.

IoT Applications: Wi-Fi modules are crucial for IoT (Internet of Things) projects. They allow your Arduino to communicate with cloud platforms, databases, and other connected devices.

Home Automation: Wi-Fi modules are commonly used in home automation projects to control lights, appliances, and other devices remotely via a smartphone or web interface.

Sensor Data Streaming: Wi-Fi modules enable you to transmit sensor data from remote locations to a central server for monitoring and analysis.

Wi-Fi modules provide connectivity and open up a world of possibilities for remote monitoring and control with Arduino projects. Depending on your project's requirements, you can choose between ESP8266 and ESP32 modules and leverage the rich libraries and resources available for these Wi-Fi-enabled Arduino platforms.

GSM/GPRS Modules: Enables cellular communication

Basic GSM/GPRS Module Setup: GSM/GPRS modules come in various forms, but common choices include the SIM800L, SIM900, and SIM800C modules. These modules require a SIM card for cellular connectivity.

SIM800L GSM/GPRS Module: To use a SIM800L module with Arduino, you can communicate with it over UART (Serial) communication. Here's a basic example of sending an SMS message

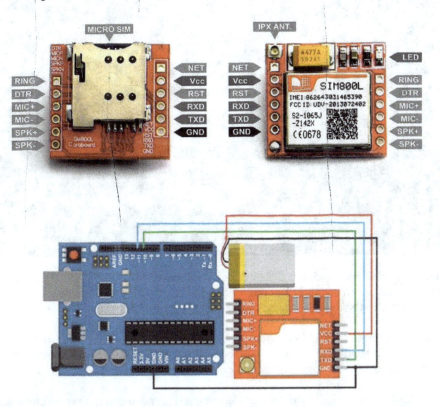

How to Interface GSM Module with Arduino

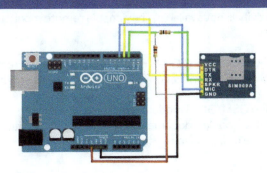

{code example 1}

```
1.  #include <SoftwareSerial.h>
2.
3.  SoftwareSerial gsmSerial(7, 8);  // RX, TX pins
4.
5.  void setup() {
6.    Serial.begin(9600);
7.    gsmSerial.begin(9600);
8.
9.    delay(1000);
10.   gsmSerial.println("AT");  // Check module communication
11.   delay(1000);
12.   gsmSerial.println("AT+CMGF=1");  // Set SMS text mode
13.   delay(1000);
14.   gsmSerial.println("AT+CMGS=\"+1234567890\"");  // Replace with the recipient's
      phone number
15.   delay(1000);
16.   gsmSerial.print("Hello, this is an Arduino SMS!");
17.   delay(1000);
18.   gsmSerial.write(26);  // Send Ctrl+Z to indicate the end of the SMS
19. }
20.
21. void loop() {
22.   // Your GSM-enabled Arduino code here...
23. }
```

SIM900 and Other Modules: Other GSM/GPRS modules like the SIM900 series require similar serial communication, but the AT commands and procedures may vary slightly. Always refer to the module's datasheet and documentation for specific details.

Internet Connectivity: GSM/GPRS modules can be used to establish internet connections. You can send HTTP requests and receive data from web services, making them suitable for IoT applications that require cellular connectivity.

Voice Calls: GSM/GPRS modules can also be used to make and receive voice calls. You can control call functions using AT commands.

IoT Applications: GSM/GPRS modules are commonly used in IoT projects where Wi-Fi or Ethernet connectivity is not available. They enable remote monitoring and control over cellular networks.

Security and Notifications: GSM/GPRS modules are useful for creating security systems that send SMS alerts or notifications in case of intrusions or other events.

Remember that using GSM/GPRS modules often involves dealing with AT commands and understanding the module's documentation thoroughly. Additionally, you'll need a SIM card with an active cellular plan to use these modules for communication over the cellular network.

LCD Displays: Displays information using text and graphics.

LCD (Liquid Crystal Display) modules are widely used in Arduino projects to display text and graphics, providing a user-friendly interface for various applications. These modules are available in different sizes and types, including character LCDs (e.g., 16×2, 20×4) and graphical LCDs (e.g., Nokia 5110, SSD1306). Here's how you can use LCD displays with Arduino:

Character LCD Displays (e.g., 16×2, 20×4): These displays are ideal for displaying alphanumeric characters and are commonly used for simple text-based interfaces.

{code example 1}

```
1.   #include <LiquidCrystal.h>
2.
3.   LiquidCrystal lcd(12, 11, 5, 4, 3, 2); // Initialize the LCD
4.
5.   void setup() {
6.     lcd.begin(16, 2); // Set the number of columns and rows (16×2)
7.     lcd.print("Hello, Arduino!"); // Display text
8.   }
9.
10.  void loop() {
11.    // Your LCD-enabled Arduino code here...
12.  }
```

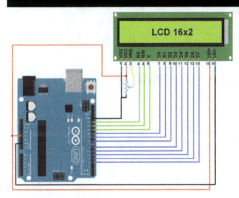

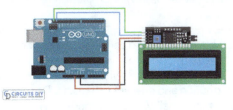

Interfacing
16x2 I2C LCD with Arduino UNO

Graphical LCD Displays (e.g., Nokia 5110, SSD1306): These displays provide more flexibility for creating graphics and custom interfaces.

For the Nokia 5110 display, you can use the "Adafruit_PCD8544" library:

{code example 2}

```
1.  #include <Adafruit_PCD8544.h>
2.
3.  Adafruit_PCD8544 display = Adafruit_PCD8544(7, 6, 5, 4, 3); // Pins for the Nokia
    5110 display
4.
5.  void setup() {
6.    display.begin();
7.    display.setContrast(50); // Adjust contrast (0-127)
8.    display.clearDisplay(); // Clear the screen
9.    display.setTextSize(1); // Text size
10.   display.setTextColor(BLACK); // Text color
11.   display.setCursor(0, 0); // Set cursor position
12.   display.println("Hello, Arduino!"); // Display text
13.   display.display(); // Show the content
14. }
15.
16. void loop() {
17.   // Your LCD-enabled Arduino code here...
18. }
```

Custom Graphics and Animation: Graphical LCDs allow you to draw custom graphics, create animations, and design unique user interfaces. You can display sensor data, graphs, icons, and more.

Scrolling Text: You can make text scroll horizontally or vertically on the display to show long messages.

Menu Systems: LCD displays are commonly used for creating menu systems in Arduino projects, where users can navigate and select options.

Sensor Data Display: You can use LCD displays to show real-time data from sensors, such as temperature, humidity, or distance.

Status Indicators: LCD displays are useful for indicating the status of various components or systems in your project.

Time and Date Display: LCD displays can show the current time and date, making them suitable for clock and calendar applications.

LCD displays provide a visual interface for your Arduino projects, allowing you to present information and interact with users. Depending on your project's requirements and desired functionality, you can choose the appropriate LCD display type and library to meet your needs.

OLED Displays: Organic LED displays with high contrast.

OLED (Organic Light Emitting Diode) displays are popular for Arduino projects due to their high contrast, wide viewing angles, and ability to display vibrant colors and crisp text and graphics. These displays come in various sizes and can be used for various applications. Here's how you can use OLED displays with Arduino:

Basic OLED Display Setup: OLED displays are available in different resolutions, such as 128×64 or 128×32 pixels. One commonly used OLED library is the "Adafruit_SSD1306" library.

{code example 1}

```
1.    #include <Adafruit_GFX.h>
2.    #include <Adafruit_SSD1306.h>
3.
4.    #define SCREEN_WIDTH 128
5.    #define SCREEN_HEIGHT 64
6.
7.    // Initialize the OLED display
8.    Adafruit_SSD1306 display(SCREEN_WIDTH, SCREEN_HEIGHT, &Wire, -1);
9.
10.   void setup() {
11.     // Initialize with I2C address 0×3D (or 0×3C for some displays)
12.     if (!display.begin(SSD1306_I2C_ADDRESS, OLED_RESET)) {
13.       Serial.println(F("SSD1306 allocation failed"));
14.       for (;;);
15.     }
16.
17.     // Clear the display buffer
18.     display.clearDisplay();
19.
20.     // Display text or graphics
21.     display.setTextSize①;
22.     display.setTextColor(SSD1306_WHITE);
23.     display.setCursor(0, 0);
24.     display.println(F("Hello, Arduino!"));
25.     display.display(); // Show the content
26.   }
27.
28.   void loop() {
29.     // Your OLED-enabled Arduino code here....
30.   }
```

Graphics and Animation: OLED displays support graphics and animation. You can draw shapes, lines, text, images, and even create animations frame by frame.

Custom Fonts: You can use custom fonts to display text in various styles and sizes, making it suitable for various applications, including clock displays and sensor data readouts.

Scrolling Text: Like other displays, you can make text scroll horizontally or vertically to show long messages.

Sensor Data Display: OLED displays are ideal for showing real-time data from sensors, making them suitable for applications like weather stations or fitness trackers.

Menu Systems: You can create interactive menu systems for user navigation and selection.

Status Indicators: OLED displays can be used for indicating the status of various components or systems in your project.

Battery-Powered Devices: OLED displays consume less power compared to traditional LCD displays, making them suitable for battery-powered devices.

OLED displays offer high-quality visual output and are a popular choice for projects requiring compact and low-power displays with excellent contrast and readability. The specific library and code you use may vary based on the OLED display model and interface (I2C or SPI) you choose.

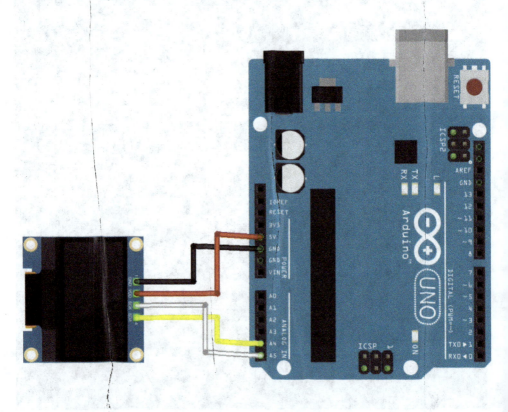

Relay Modules: Controls high-power devices.

Relay modules are essential components in Arduino projects that enable you to control high-power devices or circuits using low-power signals from the Arduino. They work as an electrically operated switch, allowing you to control devices such as lights, motors, heaters, and more. Here's how you can use relay modules with Arduino:

Relay Basics: A relay consists of an electromagnetic coil and one or more sets of contacts. When you apply a voltage to the coil (usually 5V or 12V), it creates a magnetic field that pulls the contacts together or releases them, depending on the type of relay (normally open or normally closed).

Relay Modules: Relay modules are pre-packaged relays with the necessary circuitry for protection and easy interfacing with microcontrollers like Arduino. They typically come with three or four pins: VCC (power supply), GND (ground), IN (control input), and sometimes COM (common) and NO/NC (normally open/normally closed) contacts.

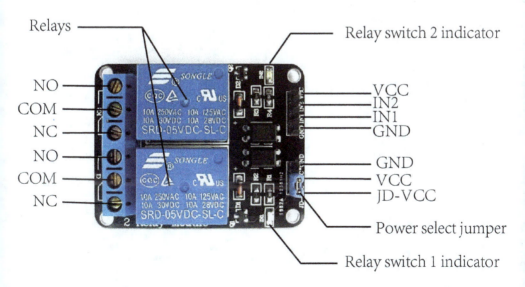

Arduino Code for Relay Control:

To control the relay, you'll typically use the digitalWrite() function to set the control pin to HIGH or LOW.

A HIGH signal activates the relay (closes the switch), while a LOW signal deactivates it (opens the switch).

Here's a simple example of controlling a relay module to switch a high-power device on and off:

{code example 1}

```
1.    const int relayPin = 2; // Digital pin where the relay module's control pin is connected
2.
3.    void setup() {
4.      pinMode(relayPin, OUTPUT); // Set the relay pin as an output
5.    }
6.
7.    void loop() {
8.      // Turn the relay on (closes the switch)
9.      digitalWrite(relayPin, HIGH);
10.    delay(2000); // Keep it on for 2 seconds
11.
12.    // Turn the relay off (opens the switch)
13.    digitalWrite(relayPin, LOW);
14.    delay(2000); // Keep it off for 2 seconds
15.  }
```

In this example, when you set the relayPin to HIGH, it activates the relay and closes the switch, allowing current to flow through the connected high-power device. Setting it to LOW deactivates the relay and opens the switch, turning off the device.

Remember to choose the appropriate relay module based on the voltage and current requirements of your high-power device. Also, ensure that you're handling high-power electrical circuits safely, following proper wiring practices and safety precautions.

Pressure Sensors: Measures pressure levels.

Pressure sensors are electronic devices used to measure and monitor pressure levels in various applications. They are valuable tools in Arduino projects, particularly for applications like weather monitoring, altitude sensing, industrial automation, and more. Pressure sensors come in various types, including:

Types of Pressure Sensors:
Analog Pressure Sensors: These sensors provide an analog voltage or current output that varies in proportion to the applied pressure. Common types include piezoresistive, capacitive, and piezoelectric sensors.

Digital Pressure Sensors: These sensors provide a digital output and often have built-in analog-to-digital converters (ADCs) for easy interfacing with microcontrollers like Arduino. Examples include I2C and SPI-based pressure sensors.

Wiring Pressure Sensors:
Analog sensors typically have three pins: power (Vcc), ground (GND), and the analog output signal (OUT).
Digital sensors may have additional pins for communication (e.g., SDA and SCL for I2C). Always check the datasheet of your specific sensor for its pinout and electrical characteristics.

Analog Pressure Sensor Example:
Connect the sensor's Vcc pin to a 5V power source, the GND pin to ground, and the OUT pin to an analog input pin on the Arduino.

Digital Pressure Sensor Example:
Connect the sensor's Vcc pin to a 5V power source, the GND pin to ground, and the communication pins (e.g., SDA and SCL for I2C) to the corresponding Arduino pins. Install any necessary libraries for the specific sensor type and follow the manufacturer's instructions for reading data.

Arduino Code:
To read data from an analog pressure sensor, you can use the analogRead() function. For digital pressure sensors, you'll typically use a library provided by the sensor manufacturer.
Here's a basic example using an analog pressure sensor (e.g., a piezoresistive pressure sensor) connected to an Arduino:

{code example 1}

```
1.   const int pressureSensorPin = A0; // Analog pin where the pressure sensor is connected
2.
3.   void setup() {
4.     Serial.begin(9600); // Initialize serial communication for debugging
5.   }
6.
7.   void loop() {
8.     // Read analog value from pressure sensor
9.     int sensorValue = analogRead(pressureSensorPin);
10.
11.    // Convert analog value to pressure (adjust based on sensor characteristics)
12.    float pressure = map(sensorValue, 0, 1023, 0, 100); // Example mapping
13.
14.    // Print pressure value to the serial monitor
15.    Serial.print("Pressure (psi): ");
16.    Serial.println(pressure);
17.
18.    delay(1000); // Delay for 1 second before the next reading
19.  }
```

In this example, the analog value from the pressure sensor is mapped to a pressure value and then displayed on the serial monitor.

Remember to adjust the code and calibration factors according to the specifications provided by the sensor's datasheet. Different pressure sensors may have different voltage-output characteristics and calibration requirements.

Water Level Sensors: Detects water levels.

Water level sensors are commonly used in Arduino projects to detect the presence or absence of water and measure the water level in a container. They are widely applied in various applications, including automatic water-level controllers, aquarium monitoring systems, and industrial processes. Here's how you can use water level sensors with Arduino:

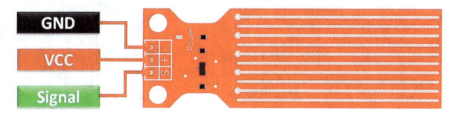

Types of Water Level Sensors:
Float Sensors: These sensors have a float that rises or falls with the water level. When the float reaches a certain point, it activates a switch, indicating the water level.

Capacitive Sensors: Capacitive sensors detect water level by measuring changes in capacitance caused by the presence of water. They are often used in non-contact applications.

Ultrasonic Sensors: Ultrasonic sensors emit sound waves that bounce off the water surface and return to the sensor. By measuring the time it takes for the waves to return, you can calculate the water level.

Conductive Sensors: Conductive sensors use the conductivity of water to detect its presence. When the sensor's electrodes come into contact with water, it completes an electrical circuit.

Wiring the Water Level Sensor:

The wiring depends on the type of sensor you are using. Always refer to the datasheet or product documentation for specific wiring instructions.
Generally, you will need to connect the sensor's power (Vcc), ground (GND), and signal pins to corresponding pins on the Arduino.
Some sensors may require additional components, such as pull-up resistors or voltage dividers, for proper operation.
Arduino Code:
*   The code for reading water level sensors varies based on the type of sensor and its output.
*   For digital sensors (e.g., float switches or capacitive sensors), you may use the digitalRead() function to check the state (HIGH or LOW) of the sensor.
*   For analog sensors (e.g., ultrasonic sensors), you can use the analogRead() function to read the sensor's output value.

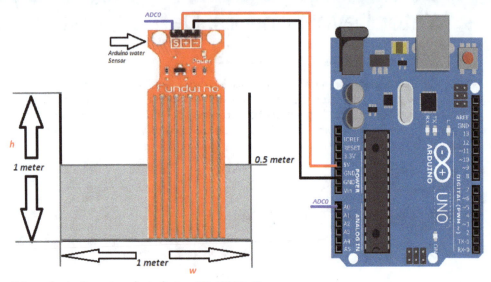

Figure labels: ADC0, Arduino water Sensor, S + -, Funduino, Power, h, 1 meter, 0.5 meter, 1 meter, w, ADC0

Volume of water in a rectangular tank = Length*width*depth

Here's a basic example using a float switch connected to an Arduino to detect the water level:

{code example 1}

```
1.  const int floatSwitchPin = 2; // Digital pin where the float switch is connected
2.
3.  void setup() {
4.    pinMode(floatSwitchPin, INPUT_PULLUP); // Set the float switch pin as an input with pull-up
      resistor
5.    Serial.begin(9600); // Initialize serial communication for debugging
6.  }
7.
8.  void loop() {
9.    // Read the state of the float switch
10.   int waterLevel = digitalRead(floatSwitchPin);
11.
12.   if (waterLevel == LOW) {
13.     Serial.println("Water level is LOW."); // Water is present
14.   } else {
15.     Serial.println("Water level is HIGH."); // No water
16.   }
17.
18.   delay(1000); // Delay for 1 second before the next reading
19. }
```

In this example, when the float switch is immersed in water, it completes the circuit, and the digital input reads LOW. When there's no water, the input reads HIGH.

Always ensure that you choose the appropriate type of water level sensor for your specific application, considering factors such as the type of liquid, environmental conditions, and the desired accuracy of water level measurement.

Voltage Sensors: Measures voltage levels

Voltage sensors, also known as voltage detectors or voltage sensors, are electronic devices used to measure and monitor voltage levels in electrical circuits. They are often used in Arduino projects for tasks such as monitoring battery voltage, measuring power supply voltage, or creating voltage-based alarms. Here's how you can use voltage sensors with Arduino:

Types of Voltage Sensors:
Analog Voltage Sensors: These sensors provide an analog output voltage that is directly proportional to the voltage being measured. They are simple to use with Arduino's analog inputs.

Digital Voltage Sensors: Some voltage sensors provide a digital output, often using I2C or SPI communication protocols. They have built-in analog-to-digital converters (ADCs) and may offer higher accuracy and resolution.

Wiring Voltage Sensors:
* The wiring of voltage sensors depends on the type and model you are using. Always refer to the datasheet or product documentation for specific wiring instructions.
* Analog voltage sensors typically have three pins: power (Vcc), ground (GND), and the analog output signal (OUT). Connect them to corresponding pins on the Arduino.
* Digital voltage sensors may require you to connect communication pins (e.g., SDA and SCL for I2C) to the corresponding Arduino pins.

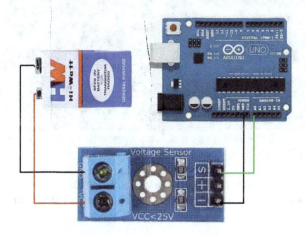

Arduino Code:

- The code for reading voltage sensors varies based on the type of sensor and its output.
- For analog voltage sensors, you can use the analogRead() function to read the sensor's output value.
- For digital voltage sensors, you may need to include a specific library provided by the sensor manufacturer and follow their instructions for reading data.

Here's a basic example using an analog voltage sensor (e.g., a simple voltage divider) to measure a voltage level:

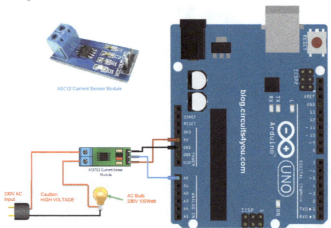

{code example 1}

```
1.   const int voltageSensorPin = A0; // Analog pin where the voltage sensor is connected
2.
3.   void setup() {
4.     pinMode(voltageSensorPin, INPUT); // Set the voltage sensor pin as an input
5.     Serial.begin(9600); // Initialize serial communication for debugging
6.   }
7.
8.   void loop() {
9.     // Read analog value from the voltage sensor
10.    int sensorValue = analogRead(voltageSensorPin);
11.
12.    // Convert analog value to voltage (adjust based on sensor characteristics)
13.    float voltage = (sensorValue / 1023.0) * 5.0; // Example calculation
14.
15.    // Print voltage value to the serial monitor
16.    Serial.print("Voltage (V): ");
17.    Serial.println(voltage, 2); // Display voltage with 2 decimal places
18.
19.    delay(1000); // Delay for 1 second before the next reading
20. }
```

In this example, the analog value from the voltage sensor is converted to a voltage value using a simple calculation. The voltage is then displayed on the serial monitor.

Always ensure that you choose the appropriate voltage sensor for your specific application, considering factors such as the voltage range you need to measure and the accuracy of the sensor.

Current Sensors: Measures current in a circuit.

Current sensors, also known as current transducers or current monitors, are electronic devices used to measure and monitor the flow of electric current in a circuit. They are valuable components in various Arduino projects, especially those involving power management, energy monitoring, or safety. Here's how you can use current sensors with Arduino:

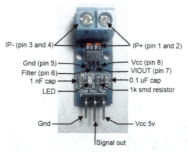

Types of Current Sensors:

- **Hall Effect Current Sensors:** These sensors use the Hall Effect to measure current. They can be non-invasive (clamped around a conductor) or integrated into a circuit. Hall Effect sensors provide a voltage output that is proportional to the current passing through them.

- **Current Shunt Resistors:** Current shunt resistors are low-resistance resistors placed in series with the circuit being measured. The voltage drop across the shunt resistor is proportional to the current. These are typically used with an amplifier to measure the voltage accurately.

- **Hall Effect Current Sensors with Built-in Amplifiers:** Some Hall Effect current sensors come with built-in amplifiers, simplifying the process of interfacing with an Arduino.

Wiring Current Sensors:

- The wiring of current sensors depends on the type and model you are using. Always refer to the datasheet or product documentation for specific wiring instructions.
- Hall Effect sensors usually have three pins: power (Vcc), ground (GND), and the output signal (OUT). Connect them to the corresponding pins on the Arduino.
- Current shunt resistors may require you to connect the voltage measurement points to an analog input pin on the Arduino.

Arduino Code:
The code for reading current sensors depends on the type of sensor and its output.
For Hall Effect sensors with analog output, you can use the analogRead() function to read the sensor's output voltage.
For Hall Effect sensors with built-in amplifiers, the code may vary depending on the sensor model. Some sensors may have libraries provided by the manufacturer.
Current shunt resistors require an amplifier circuit to accurately measure voltage drop. You can use an instrumentation amplifier or an operational amplifier (op-amp) to amplify the voltage across the shunt resistor.

Here's a basic example using a Hall Effect current sensor with an analog output to measure current:

{code example 1}

```
1.   const int currentSensorPin = A0; // Analog pin where the current sensor is connected
2.
3.   void setup() {
4.     pinMode(currentSensorPin, INPUT); // Set the current sensor pin as an input
5.     Serial.begin(9600); // Initialize serial communication for debugging
6.   }
7.
8.   void loop() {
9.     // Read analog value from the current sensor
10.    int sensorValue = analogRead(currentSensorPin);
11.
12.    // Convert analog value to current (adjust based on sensor characteristics)
13.    float current = (sensorValue / 1023.0) * maxCurrent; // Example calculation
14.
15.    // Print current value to the serial monitor
16.    Serial.print("Current (A): ");
17.    Serial.println(current, 2); // Display current with 2 decimal places
18.
19.    delay(1000); // Delay for 1 second before the next reading
20. }
```

In this example, the analog value from the current sensor is converted to a current value using a simple calculation. The current is then displayed on the serial monitor.

Always ensure that you choose the appropriate current sensor for your specific application, considering factors such as the maximum current you need to measure and the accuracy of the sensor. Additionally, be cautious when working with high-current circuits and follow proper safety precautions.

Refference

- **setup() and loop() Functions:**

setup(): This function is called once when the Arduino starts. It's typically used for setting up initial configurations, pin modes, and hardware.

```
1.   void setup() {
2.     // Initialization code goes here
3.   }
```

loop(): This function is called repeatedly after the setup() function. It contains the main program logic and runs indefinitely.

```
1.   void loop() {
2.     // Main program logic goes here
3.   }
```

- **Pin Configuration:**

pinMode(pin, mode): Sets the mode of a digital pin as INPUT or OUTPUT.

```
1.   pinMode(13, OUTPUT); // Set pin 13 as an output
```

- **Digital I/O:**

digitalWrite(pin, value): Writes a digital HIGH or LOW value to a pin set as an OUTPUT.

```
1.   digitalWrite(13, HIGH); // Set pin 13 to HIGH (ON)
2.
```

- **Digital I/O:**

digitalRead(pin): Reads the digital value (HIGH or LOW) from a pin set as an INPUT.

```
1.   int buttonState = digitalRead(2); // Read the state of pin 2
```

analogWrite(pin, value): Generates a PWM (Pulse Width Modulation) signal on a pin set as an OUTPUT, creating an analog-like output voltage (0-255).

```
1.   analogWrite(9, 128); // Generate a PWM signal on pin 9 with a 50% duty cycle
```

72

www.ingramcontent.com/pod-product-compliance
Lightning Source LLC
LaVergne TN
LVHW051741050326
832903LV00023B/1040